AMERICA IN WORLD WAR II

1942

AMERICA
IN WORLD
WAR II

EDWARD F. DOLAN

THE MILLBROOK PRESS
BROOKFIELD, CONNECTICUT

Maps by Joe Le Monnier

Cover photograph courtesy of Photri

All photographs courtesy of the National Archives except
for Photri: pp. 6, 38; UPI/Bettmann: pp. 21 (top), 32;
Wide World: p. 51 (top left); King Features Syndicate,
Inc. (Reprinted with special permission); p. 62.

Cataloging-in-Publication Data

Dolan, Edward F.
America in World War II: 1942 / by Edward F. Dolan.

p. cm
Bibliography: p.
Includes index
Summary: A history of the United States in the first
battles of World War II, when it was unprepared for war
and suffered many defeats but also won a few victories.
ISBN 1-56294-007-4
1. United States — History — 1933-1945.   2. World
War, 1939-1945 — United States.   3. World War,
1939-1945 — Pacific Ocean.   4. Japan — History
— 1868-1945.   I. Title.   II. Series
940.54   1991

CONTENTS

INTRODUCTION: THE STORY THUS FAR

World War II erupted in Europe in September 1939, when German dictator Adolf Hitler unleashed his armies to conquer Poland. Germany's close ally, Italy, joined Hitler in the war a year later.

The United States, though angered by the German attack, stayed out of the fighting. It did so because vast numbers of its people and many of its national leaders wanted nothing to do with foreign conflicts. They remembered with deep sorrow the deaths and wounds that their countrymen suffered in World War I.

At the same time that Hitler's armies were on the march, Japan was continuing its war against China. That war had begun in 1931, when Japan had set out to become the dominant power in Asia by invading the Chinese region of Manchuria.

The United States stayed out of the war until December 7, 1941. On that day, the Japanese launched surprise attacks against six American military installations on the Hawaiian island of Oahu, chief among them the giant naval base at Pearl Harbor. At the same time, the Japanese struck elsewhere in the Pacific. They attacked American bases in the

**German dictator
Adolf Hitler**

Philippine islands and on the islands of Wake, Guam, and Midway. Also hit were the British forces in Malaya and in Hong Kong.

The attacks were meant to cripple the Americans and British so that they would be powerless to stop Japan from invading Malaya and the East Indies (today called Indonesia). Both Malaya and the East Indies were rich in natural resources, especially oil, rubber, and metals, that Japan sorely needed for its war machine.

On December 8, 1941, an angry United States declared war on Japan. Japan's fellow powers—Germany and Italy—then declared war on the United States. The United States answered with a return declaration. Great Britain, which was already at war with Germany and Italy, joined the United States in the fight against the Japanese.

The new year, 1942, saw America battling one enemy in the Pacific and another in Europe and Africa. We turn first to the Pacific, beginning with the fighting in the Philippines. To see all that went on there, we must go back to December 1941.

ONE:
THE RETREAT
TO BATAAN

December 1941 was a terrible month for the Philippine islands. It began with Japanese air strikes against U.S. bases on the main island of Luzon. Then Japanese forces invaded Luzon and began to battle their way toward Manila, the capital city of the Philippines. The month ended with American and Filipino troops digging in near Manila for a last-ditch stand against the Japanese.

At the time of the Japanese attacks, the Philippines, which had been won from Spain in the Spanish-American War (1898), were the largest of America's holdings in the Pacific. They were also just five years away from realizing a dream long held by the Philippine people. In 1934, the United States had agreed to grant the Philippines its independence at the end of a twelve-year period—in 1946.

The Philippines consists of more than 7,000 islands of all sizes. The largest is Luzon. Blanketed with jungle lands and swamps, it is about as big as the state of Ohio. Near its southern tip lies giant Manila Bay. The city of Manila stands on the shores of the bay.

THE AIR STRIKES ▪ Several hours after the devastation of Pearl Harbor far out in the Pacific, fifty-four Japanese bombers roared in over Luzon and loosed their deadly loads on two air bases near Manila—Clark and Iba airfields. Before the American pilots could dash to their planes and get into the air to fight back, dozens of planes exploded in flames. At least fifty-six fighters, eighteen B-17 bombers, and twenty-five other aircraft were destroyed. This was more than half the number of U.S. warplanes on the islands.

The next Japanese air strike came on December 9. This time the target was the Cavite naval base, located on Manila Bay, just outside the city of Manila. Bombs rained down on the ships of the U.S. Asiatic Fleet, a force consisting mainly of cruisers and destroyers.

By a stroke of good luck, most of the vessels in the Asiatic Fleet were away at the time. As bombs hit all around him, the fleet commander, Admiral Thomas C. Hart, quickly put the rest of his ships out to sea. They sailed on to Java, where they would take part in future fighting.

THE INVASION AT LINGAYEN GULF ▪ But that was all the good luck the month would bring. On December 20, the Japanese invaded and began to take over the island of Mindanao to the south of Luzon. The next day, they struck an even heavier blow. The 100,000-man Japanese 14th Army sailed into Lingayen Gulf and stormed ashore on Luzon itself. The gulf is a finger of water that knifes its way into the west side of the island. It lies just 110 miles north of Manila. General Masaharu Homma, the commander of the enemy army, was under orders from the war chiefs in Tokyo to capture Manila and bring all of Luzon to its knees in fifty days.

General Homma knew that the Philippine islands were defended by three forces that totaled about 135,000 men spread

THE
PHILIPPINES

*South
China Sea*

*Sulu
Sea*

Philippine Sea

Luzon

Laoag ●
Aparri ●
Tuguegarao ●
Vigan ●
Ilagan ●

Lingayen Gulf

Clark Airfield ○
Ibu Airfield ○
Manila Bay
Manila ●
Bataan
Corregidor
Cavite ●
Lamon Bay

Mindoro

Sibuyan Sea

Masbate Samar

Panay
Bacolod ●
Cebu
Cebu ●
Leyte

Palawan

Negros
Bohol

Bohol Sea

Mindanao
Davao ●

Moro Gulf
Davao Gulf

Jan 6

BATAAN
PENINSULA

Olongapo ●

△ *Mt. Samat*
Abucay ●
△ *Mt. Santa Rosa*
Moron ●
Mauban ●
Pilar ●
Orion ●

△ *Mt. Bataan*

1ST CORPS
(Wainright)
△ **2ND CORPS**
(Parker)

*Surrender
April 9*

Mariveles ●
Cabcaben ●

△ =Mountain
Corregidor

0 10 Miles

throughout the islands. The largest of the three was the Philippine Army, which was made up of about 100,000 Filipino soldiers. Next, there was a U.S. infantry division of 20,000 men. Finally, there was the unit known as the Philippine Scouts. This was manned by 10,000 rugged Filipino fighters who served as part of the American Army. The three forces were commanded by General Douglas MacArthur, who was preparing them to defend the islands when independence was to come, in 1946.

It was a confident Homma who sent his men ashore at Lingayen Gulf. He felt certain that he would have no trouble besting MacArthur's forces, especially those from the newly formed Philippine Army. Homma knew that they were still far from being fully trained. He felt they would be no match for his battle-toughened soldiers, who had fought long and hard in his nation's war with China.

Homma was right. The beaches at Lingayen were defended by only four divisions of the Philippine Army. Bombers were sent streaking in over the Filipino troops. Warships raked them with shells and machine-gun bullets. Tanks, artillery, and infantrymen poured ashore. Most of the Filipino soldiers fled in terror.

But the Philippine Scouts and the U.S. soldiers remained and courageously battled the invaders. However, they were soon overwhelmed by the enemy and began to fall back. On December 22, a message reached General MacArthur's headquarters in Manila. It said that all of Homma's army was ashore and pushing toward the city.

More bad news arrived the next day. A second Japanese force was landing at Lamon Bay, some sixty miles to the south of Manila. The invaders were now closing in on the city from two sides.

General Homma (left) and his forces land on the island of Luzon in Lingayen Gulf on December 21, 1941.

MACARTHUR TAKES ACTION ▪ MacArthur immediately sent a message to his two field commanders, Major Generals Jonathan M. Wainwright and George M. Parker. Wainwright was the American officer in charge of the forces at Lingayen; Parker commanded the troops at Lamon Bay. MacArthur told them to pull their men out and head for Bataan, a peninsula of swamp and jungle north of the entrance to Manila Bay. The troops were to set up strong defensive positions there to stage a last-ditch stand against the invaders.

MacArthur also decided to move his headquarters out to the small and heavily fortified island of Corregidor, which stands near the entrance to Manila Bay. From there, he would direct the battle against the Japanese. With luck, his troops could hold out until reinforcements arrived from the United States. He told his staff officers that if help failed to come, he would remain at his post until captured or killed. (Reinforcements never did come. Faced with enemies on two sides of the world and new to the fighting, the United States was not in a position to send them.)

MacArthur had a definite reason for moving his troops to Bataan and his headquarters to Corregidor—he knew that he could not defend Manila. It was about to be hit hard, and he had lost almost all his warplanes in the air strikes on Clark and Iba fields and in the fighting of the past days. So his plan was to let the Japanese have Manila itself, but to keep them from using Manila Bay as a military base for as long as possible. He was sure the guns on Bataan and Corregidor could prevent them from entering the giant bay for weeks at least.

The next days were hectic ones for Major Generals Wainwright and Parker. To reach Bataan, Parker had to move his men northward past Manila and then around the upper end of Manila Bay. This meant that Wainwright's troops had to hold back the hard-charging Japanese long enough to allow Parker's forces to complete the trip.

Wainwright halted his troops just under a hundred miles from Manila. He ordered them to dig in. The defensive line took shape on December 24. It held for two days before enemy tanks came crashing through. Wainwright's men began to retreat. But they fell back as slowly as they could, to give Parker's men the time they needed to reach Bataan. Repeatedly, they tried to slow the Japanese with attacks of their own.

Meanwhile, Parker's troops were steadily moving north. MacArthur sent army trucks to pick them up and speed them along. But there were not enough trucks for all the troops. So MacArthur took over every civilian vehicle he could find—including private cars, taxicabs, and the city's brightly colored buses. They hurried south to Parker's men and then swung around for the trip to Bataan.

Manila itself buzzed with activity. Army and Navy men worked to remove all the military supplies and food from the bases around the city and get them to Bataan and Corregidor. Day and night, heavily laden barges and boats scuttled back and forth across Manila Bay.

TO CORREGIDOR ▪ At dusk on that Christmas Eve, General MacArthur left his headquarters at Manila and went aboard the small steamer *Don Esteban* for the trip to Corregidor. With him were his staff officers and his wife and four-year-old son.

Thunderous explosions tore through the evening air. The

Japanese were closing in so quickly that there was little time left to move more food and supplies out of the city. Military supplies that had to be left behind were blown up so that they would not fall into enemy hands. Food that could not be moved was left for the Filipino people. To the south, giant clouds of black smoke rose into the sky as more than a million gallons of oil at the Cavite naval base were being put to the torch.

At a little after 9 o'clock that night, MacArthur stepped off the *Don Esteban* and onto the small island that was nick-named "the Rock." The general immediately settled into his new headquarters.

On January 2, 1942, MacArthur heard that the Japanese were pouring into Manila and taking command of the city. Then came the word that Wainwright and Parker had completed their moves to Bataan. Of the 28,000 soldiers who had been with Wainwright at Lingayen Gulf, only 12,000 remained. His losses had been great, and several thousand of his Philippine troops had deserted him. Some had left out of fear, and others because they secretly hated the Americans. Major General Parker had started with 15,000 soldiers. He now had 14,000. Counting those men who had been working behind the front lines during the retreat, there were just over 80,000 troops on the peninsula. Crowded in among them were more than 20,000 of the Filipino people who lived on Bataan.

The two major generals set up a line of defense across the upper end of the peninsula and waited for the approaching Japanese. The battle for Bataan, a strip of land about twenty miles wide and twenty-five miles long, was about to begin.

commander desperately tried to move his troops back to their own lines, but only 377 of his 1,000 men escaped death.

Regardless of this victory, life worsened each day for the defending troops on Bataan. They had sufficient ammunition, but they were growing weak from hunger as their food supplies began to run out. (In part, the rations ran low because they were being used to feed not only the troops but also the Filipino people who lived on Bataan.) To avoid starvation, the Philippine Scouts killed and ate their horses. They also ate whatever animals they could find in the jungle, including dogs, snakes, and monkeys.

The United States tried to bring food to the peninsula. Ships and submarines laden with supplies made their way to Bataan from Australia. However, except for three ships and a few subs, they were captured or sunk by Japanese warships that had set up a blockade along the western coast of Bataan and across the entrance to Manila Bay.

The lack of food was not the only problem facing the defenders. Medical supplies were also running low, especially their store of quinine, a drug used to combat the tropical disease malaria. Many of the men were falling ill with malaria and two other tropical illnesses, beriberi and dengue fever. Many were also suffering from dysentery.

General Homma's men were in no better condition. They, too, were ill and exhausted. The general was worried. The Bataan peninsula had been more strongly defended than he had expected. By mid-February, he had run out of the fifty days he had been given to take Luzon. More than 7,000 of his men had been killed in the fighting, and several thousand more had been wounded. Some 12,000 were down with tropical illnesses.

Knowing that his men were no longer fit to take Bataan by themselves, Homma asked that fresh soldiers be sent to him. While awaiting their arrival, he rested his troops.

MARCH AND APRIL ▪ Though not attempting to openly attack in March, Homma tried another tactic. He sent some of his best fighters sneaking through the U.S. lines in ones and twos. When enough men were behind the lines, they assembled in small groups and did as much harm as possible. They set fire to ammunition dumps and ambushed truck convoys. They stole into campsites at night and knifed the sleeping men to death.

On March 10, MacArthur summoned Major General Wainwright to Corregidor. He told Wainwright that he, MacArthur, had been ordered by President Franklin D. Roosevelt to leave the tiny island and travel to Australia so that he could be of use later in the war. From now on, Wainwright would be in command in the Philippines. Major General Edward P. King, Jr., was to take his place in the field.

MAJ. GEN. EDWARD P. KING, JR.
MAJ. GEN. GEORGE M. PARKER

King and Parker were the field commanders during the final days of fighting on Bataan. King replaced Wainwright in the field after Wainwright went to Corregidor and took command of the entire Philippines.

MacArthur told Wainwright not to surrender but to fight on to the very last man.

Two nights later, MacArthur, his family, and his staff boarded four PT boats. Under the cover of darkness, the boats sneaked past the Japanese warships blockading Manila Bay and sped south to the island of Mindanao. From there, he and his party flew to Australia.

On landing in Australia, MacArthur issued a statement to the people of the United States and the Philippines. In it, he said: "I have come through and I shall return."

Those words, "I shall return," soon became a battle cry in the Pacific. But they did not inspire the troops on Bataan. Rather, the men greeted the words with anger.

The troops felt they had good reason for their anger. Most had never liked MacArthur. They had always thought him a cold man who cared little for his soldiers. Only once since the Japanese invasion had he come to see how they were faring in the field. The rest of the time he had remained in his underground headquarters on Corregidor, a fact that had earned him the nickname "Dugout Doug." Now they felt he had abandoned them by going to Australia.

MacArthur really had wanted to remain on Corregidor until the very end. Officials in Washington, D.C., had sent him numerous messages urging him to depart for Australia. He had ignored all the messages. It had taken a direct order from President Roosevelt to make him leave.

But there was little time for thoughts of the general's departure. On April 3, after fresh troops had arrived from Japan, General Homma at last launched his final attack. It began with a five-hour artillery barrage and air bombardment. Then the enemy force hurled itself into battle. In the next two days, two divisions of the Philippine Army were wiped out. Major General Parker's men were thrown back so far that they were in danger of being pushed into Manila Bay.

Major General King attempted a counterattack early in the fighting. It was a brave effort, but it failed. Enemy tanks and artillery, supported by gunfire from Zero fighter planes, tore the Americans to ribbons. There were no U.S. planes left to fend off the Zeros.

From Corregidor, Wainwright ordered King to try another counterattack. In keeping with MacArthur's last order before leaving for Australia, he also told King not to surrender under any circumstances.

King decided to ignore these commands. He could see that a counterattack would do no good. The men of Bataan were too sick and weak to carry it out. Unless the fighting was stopped soon, there would be no place to go but into Manila Bay.

And so, without telling Wainwright, King approached the enemy lines on April 9, holding a white flag. He met with Homma's chief field officer, Colonel Motoo Nakayama, to discuss a surrender and to ask if his men would be well treated by their captors. On hearing the question, the insulted colonel replied coldly, "We are not barbarians."

King accepted Nakayama's word with a nod. He handed over his pistol as a sign of surrender.

The U.S. and Filipino troops that survived all the fighting—some 76,000 men in all—were now in Japanese hands. The battle for Bataan was over.

THREE:
CORREGIDOR AND A
MARCH TO DEATH

One battle was over. But another began on the very day of Bataan's surrender, the battle to take Corregidor. The tiny island's capture would mark the total defeat of Luzon and allow the Japanese to use Manila Bay as a military base.

Lying about two miles off the foot of Bataan and shaped like a comma, Corregidor is an island of volcanic rock that takes up only 1,735 acres. But in 1942, those acres bristled with gun batteries, twenty-three in all. Each battery housed one or two giant twelve-inch cannons or mortars. Most were set in open pits surrounded by brick and concrete walls some fifteen feet thick. In addition, there were six anti-aircraft guns, plus numerous small artillery pieces. These guns were joined by batteries on three small islands nearby in Manila Bay.

Midway along the length of Corregidor was an area that contained docks, warehouses, fuel depots, water-storage tanks, and the island's power plant. Close by stood Malinta Hill. Drilled into the hill were more than forty connecting tunnels that together were known as the Malinta Tunnel. The tunnels, all thickly walled with concrete, housed supplies, sleeping quarters, a communications center, a hospital, and Wainwright's headquarters.

Malinta Tunnel on Corregidor was temporary headquarters to U.S. Army personnel during the Japanese invasion of the Philippines.

CORREGIDOR UNDER SIEGE ▪ As soon as Bataan fell, General Homma turned his eyes toward Corregidor. He planned to invade the island, but he did not attempt to do so immediately. Rather, knowing that Corregidor's batteries would devastate an enemy coming across the water, he first set about destroying those guns and the ones on the three nearby islands. On April 9, he began a vicious artillery barrage that lasted almost a month. Each day also brought a series of air strikes. Between April 9 and the month's end, Corregidor suffered more than a hundred air bombings.

The American batteries fired back at the enemy, adding to the awful din. But, one by one, the guns on Corregidor and the three islands were destroyed.

Corregidor itself was reduced to smoldering ruins as batteries, warehouses, offices, and docks were struck. Inside the Malinta tunnels, the concrete walls began to split open. A choking dust was created with every bursting shell, making the air almost impossible to breathe. The pipes that brought in fresh air were ruptured. Even worse, the water lines to the tunnels from Corregidor's wells were broken. There was little water left to drink and practically none for washing.

More than 13,000 troops were on Corregidor. Crowded in among them were hordes of Filipino citizens who had come from Bataan and Manila to find safety. Most of the soldiers and civilians had taken shelter in the tunnels. There was not enough food or sleeping accommodations for everyone. People lay wherever they could and nibbled at their meager rations. Daily, the air around them grew fouler with the odor of unwashed bodies and the smell of death.

On May 1, Wainwright estimated that—not counting the bombs dropped in the air raids—Corregidor had been hit by

1.8 million pounds of shells. They had knocked out all the island's large batteries except one, an emplacement of giant mortars. This was destroyed the next day when the mortars' magazine took a direct hit and blew up. The sky turned a blinding white, and the explosion shook the entire island.

With the loss of that last giant battery, Wainwright knew the end was near. Except for a few small artillery pieces and his exhausted and starving troops, Corregidor was defenseless. Homma would now strike.

The invasion came on the night of May 5. Small boats swept out of the darkness. Troops poured ashore on the narrow tail of the island, a tail that was just six hundred yards wide. For a time, they were stalled by a small force of Americans and Filipinos on guard there. But the outnumbered defenders could not hold their ground as tanks and armored cars joined the enemy charge. The Japanese began to surge toward Wainwright's headquarters. The last of Wainwright's troops, all of them weak with hunger, went out to meet the onslaught. They fought savagely but to no avail. Just four hours after landing, the Japanese had come to within a mile of the Malinta tunnels.

Wainwright decided he could no longer obey MacArthur's order to fight on to the last man. The battle must end now, before more lives were uselessly sacrificed. He placed white flags outside the entrance to the tunnels. Then he left Corregidor and traveled to Bataan to meet with General Homma.

Wainwright planned to surrender only Corregidor. But Homma demanded that all of the Philippine islands be turned over to him. He knew there were U.S. and Filipino troops on several of the other islands. Unless they were made to lay down their arms, they would plague him with guerrilla fighting for months to come.

Although Wainwright hated the idea of a total surrender, he had no choice but to agree to Homma's demands. At midnight on May 6, 1942, the major general surrendered the Philippines to the Japanese. But the story of Bataan and Corregidor was not yet over.

THE MARCH TO DEATH ▪ On April 15, as General Homma's guns were pounding Corregidor, the American and Filipino soldiers on Bataan began to be moved to prison camps. Most of them were slated for imprisonment at Camp O'Donnell, a U.S. Army base now in Japanese hands. It lay some sixty-five miles north of Bataan. In later years, when the outside world learned of the sufferings endured by the U.S. and Filipino troops during the move to O'Donnell, their journey was given a dramatic name by the American press—the Bataan Death March.

When Bataan fell, General Homma found himself with 76,000 prisoners on his hands. He had expected only 25,000 and had planned to move them by truck and rail to O'Donnell. But there were not enough trucks and freight cars for all the prisoners, and so most of them—80 percent of whom were so sick they could barely walk—were forced to hike northward along a narrow jungle trail.

Every step of the way was marked by terrible hardships. Many of the men, too weak to take another step, fell and died alongside the trail. Adding to the suffering was the cruelty of some of the Japanese guards, who made a falsehood of Colonel Nakayama's statement to Major General King that "We are not barbarians." These guards prodded the march-

A Japanese artist's portrayal of the surrender talks on Bataan between General Wainwright and General Homma.

ers along with bayonets and clubs. Stragglers were beaten to make them catch up with their comrades. When a prisoner dropped from exhaustion or illness, he was apt to be shot or bayoneted to death. One day, some guards became so infuriated with the slowness of the march that they bayoneted and beheaded some 350 men in a two-hour period.

Why these awful cruelties by some of the guards? There are several possible answers. The guards themselves may have been so sick and exhausted that their feelings toward the prisoners turned to rage. Some may simply have been brutish individuals. And some may have thought that they were acting in accordance with the Japanese military code called *bushido*. In great part, this code held that to surrender in battle was a disgrace and that any soldier who did so was not deserving of any human kindness or consideration.

After marching just over fifty miles, the prisoners came to a railhead. There they were crammed into airless boxcars for a train trip of several miles. They staggered the final seven miles to Camp O'Donnell.

These men, on the Bataan Death March, had their hands tied behind their backs! The photo shows them to be weak and exhausted—certainly no threat to the Japanese.

GEN. MASAHARU HOMMA

During and immediately after the war, Homma was widely seen as a cruel man because of the brutal Bataan Death March. This view of Homma is now considered unfair. He wanted to transport the prisoners by truck but was forced to march them because he did not have sufficient vehicles. Though not personally to blame for the cruelties of his men, he was held responsible as commander and was executed as a war criminal in 1946.

It was later estimated that the Bataan Death March had taken the lives of between 7,000 and 10,000 American and Filipino soldiers. Another 10,000, mostly Filipinos, were listed as missing.

The men on Corregidor were somewhat luckier when the island fell into Japanese hands. The surviving U.S. and Filipino troops were packed aboard small freighters and taken to Manila, to be herded through the streets to celebrate the Japanese victory. They were then placed in boxcars for a four-hour trip in the sweltering heat to a prison camp near the city of Cabanatuam. In the first two months at the camp, 2,000 prisoners died of disease and starvation.

Major General Jonathan Wainwright spent the rest of the war in a prison camp. He felt he had shamed himself by giving up the Philippines. He was certain he would be hated and scorned by his countrymen for surrendering. Instead, when set free at the end of the fighting, he found that he was a hero and that his stand at Corregidor had inspired the American people and added to their determination to win the war.

MAJ. GEN. JONATHAN M. WAINWRIGHT

Soon after his release from the Japanese prison camp at war's end in 1945, Major General Wainwright was awarded the Congressional Medal of Honor for his heroic leadership on Corregidor. Wainwright was also a veteran of World War I.

FOUR:
AMERICA STRIKES
BACK

With Wainwright's surrender, Japan held sway over more than 12.5 million square miles of land and sea in the Southwest Pacific.

All the Japanese attacks, including that on Pearl Harbor, had ended in success. The United States had lost the Philippines and the islands of Guam and Wake. The British had lost Hong Kong, Burma, and the Malayan peninsula with its large fortress at Singapore. But topping off all the conquests was the taking of the East Indies (today Indonesia), the Dutch-owned islands that offered such a wealth of oil and other raw materials needed by Japan's war machine. Invaded in March 1942, they were conquered a month later.

The Japanese leaders thought that the battered Americans and British would now ask for peace. They were astonished when they received no such request. Instead, they heard that the United States was preparing for a long war. First came the news that two commanders had been named to run the Pacific war. General MacArthur was to lead all the forces in the Southwest Pacific, an area that stretched from the Philippines to Australia. The rest of the Pacific was to be commanded by the Navy's Admiral Chester W. Nimitz.

MIDWAY
ISLANDS

Wake

PACIFIC OCEAN

MARIANA
ISLANDS
Guam

MARSHALL
ISLANDS

CAROLINE
ISLANDS

Equator

New Ireland
Rabaul
New Britain
Bouganville
PAPUA

Port Moresby
Guadacanal
SOLOMON

Coral Sea

ISLANDS

Next came word that MacArthur was building military bases in Australia and setting up a supply lane between Australia and the United States. This news caused the Japanese to act. They decided to seize a chain of islands just north of Australia. The islands would then serve as springboards for attacks on passing U.S. freighters and troopships bound for Australia.

The targets were New Britain (which the Japanese successfully invaded in February), the Solomon Islands (successfully invaded in March), and New Guinea. It was during the New Guinea invasion that the Americans really began to strike back and avenge the many defeats suffered since Pearl Harbor.

THE AIR ATTACK AT NEW GUINEA ▪ The largest of the invasion targets was New Guinea, owned partly by the Netherlands and partly by Australia. On March 8, the Japanese came ashore on the northern side of the island. Their plan was to advance overland and then capture the principal city, Port

ADM. CHESTER W. NIMITZ

In 1942, Admiral Nimitz and General MacArthur were named as the chief commanders of the Pacific forces.

Moresby, which was located on the southern coast and which would be used as a base for future attacks on Australia-bound U.S. ships. The city was guarded by a contingent of Australian and American troops.

In early 1942, the United States had four aircraft carriers in the Pacific, the *Yorktown, Lexington, Saratoga,* and *Enterprise.* (They had all been at sea and had escaped harm during the Pearl Harbor attack.) Two of the carriers—the *Yorktown* and the *Lexington*—were in the Coral Sea, which bordered on New Guinea, when the Japanese hit the island. Word of the invasion was flashed to them. They sent more than a hundred torpedo planes and dive-bombers speeding to the invasion site.

The planes found a large fleet unloading troops and supplies. They roared in and scored one direct hit after another. The jubilant pilots returned to their carriers with the news that they had sunk five supply ships and troop transports and had damaged two cruisers and a destroyer.

Compared with the harm the Japanese had already done, the victory was a small one. But it *was* a victory, something that the entire United States had needed since Pearl Harbor. Another success came within a few weeks.

THE DOOLITTLE RAID ▪ On a gray morning in April, a B-25 bomber lumbered along the flight deck of a carrier and pulled itself upward. Lieutenant Colonel James H. Doolittle sat at the controls. Fifteen B-25s followed him into the air as he banked and headed west. The mission assigned to him and his seventy-nine airmen was to bomb Japan. Theirs was to be the war's first air attack against the Japanese homeland.

For more than a month, Doolittle's men had been training in the United States for the mission. Time and again, they had practiced getting their giant planes aloft in the short distance that a carrier deck would afford them. Then the planes were hoisted aboard the Navy's new carrier, the *Hornet,* for a voyage that carried them from San Francisco to a point some five hundred miles off the Japanese coast.

On the morning of April 18, the B-25s took to the air. The bombing plan did not call for them to return to the *Hornet,* as they were unable to carry sufficient fuel for a round-trip. And so, on completing their mission, they were to fly on to friendly airfields in China.

The B-25s reached the main island of Honshu at midday. Taking the Japanese by complete surprise, they swept over their targets. Six cities were hit, chief among them Japan's capital, Tokyo, and the seaports of Yokosuka and Yokohoma. All the bombing runs were aimed at military and industrial installations. Each run was to last just a few minutes, with the planes then speeding on toward China.

Doolittle's plane takes off for the first U. S. air raid on Japan.

LT. COL. JAMES H. DOOLITTLE

Doolittle was the leader of the first air attack against Japan. He had served as a pilot in World War I and gained fame as a racing flier in the 1920s. He became an executive in the aerospace industry after World War II.

But Doolittle ran into trouble. His planes had battled headwinds all the way from the *Hornet* and had used up more fuel than he had anticipated. One by one, they ran out of fuel. Many of his men had to take to their parachutes.

Five drowned when they came down in the waters between Japan and China. Eight came down in an area of China held by Japan and were taken prisoner. Three of them were executed and a fourth died in prison.

The remaining men—including Doolittle—managed to reach safety in China and eastern Russia. They eventually worked their way back to U.S.-held territory.

The Doolittle raid did little actual damage. But it accomplished its main objective. It shocked the Japanese by showing them that America was ready to fight and that it intended to bring the fight to their own land.

THE BATTLE OF THE CORAL SEA ▪ The overland march to Port Moresby ended a few weeks after the Japanese invaded New Guinea. Responsible for its failure were two factors. First were the tropical diseases that felled the Japanese troops as they struggled across the jungle-covered mountains that separated the northern and southern sections of the island. Second was the fierce resistance put up by the defending Australian and American troops.

The Japanese retreated from the mountains. They continued to hold the northern section of New Guinea for months to come and extended their control to its western regions. But they developed a new plan for taking Port Moresby that called for the city to be invaded directly from the Coral Sea. The enemy began assembling an invasion fleet of carriers, warships, and troopships. On May 1, the advance units in the fleet set sail for New Guinea from an island to the north. They were followed by the main fleet on May 4.

Fortunately, Admiral Nimitz knew of the invasion thanks to U.S. cryptographers, who had broken the code used by the Japanese in their war messages. He ordered a task force to locate the invaders and drive them off. The force consisted of the carriers *Yorktown* and *Lexington* and a flotilla of support warships.

However, its commander, Rear Admiral Frank J. Fletcher, faced a major problem. He knew that the invasion ships were somewhere in the Coral Sea, but Nimitz was unable to give him their exact position. The job of finding them in the vast sea of 1.4 million square miles would be extremely difficult, maybe even impossible. On the enemy side, Admiral Takeo Tagaki had learned that Fletcher was hunting for him. But Tagaki shared Fletcher's problem. He, too, had no idea where his enemy was located.

REAR ADM. FRANK J. FLETCHER

Known by the nickname ''Jack,'' Fletcher not only commanded the U.S. forces in the Battle of the Coral Sea but also participated in the fighting at Midway and Guadalcanal.

During the opening days of May, the two commanders kept a sharp eye out for each other. Neither glimpsed the other's main fleet, but each sent up planes that did sight some of the other's outlying ships. One American sighting led to an attack that sank a Japanese destroyer and three minesweepers. Tagaki's planes found a U.S. destroyer and an oil supply ship. They sent the destroyer to the bottom and set the supply ship ablaze.

Next, Fletcher's planes located one of Tagaki's most important advance ships—the small carrier *Shoho*—as it drew near New Guinea. In a storm of torpedoes and bombs, the vessel burst into flames and quickly sank. It was the first Japanese carrier to be destroyed in the war.

The two admirals finally pinpointed each other's location on May 8. Their fleets were 150 miles apart. Each immediately launched air attacks and suffered heavy losses.

Fletcher's planes set the carrier *Shokau* afire and put it out of action. Japanese planes hit the *Lexington* with torpedoes and bombs. The carrier burst into flames but managed to stay afloat. When the battle ended, it began to struggle south to Australia, with a number of ships clustered protectively around it. Its crew felt certain that the ship would make it to safety.

But late in the day, the sparks from one of the ship's generators made contact with fumes escaping from a damaged fuel line. A series of deafening explosions rocked the ship. Mountains of smoke erupted from its interior. The ship began to sink, and the crew was ordered over the side. More than 2,000 sailors made their way to the surrounding ships. Then, as night fell, the burning carrier was put out of its misery by four torpedoes from one of those vessels.

Converted from a battle cruiser, the *USS Lexington* appeared to survive the torpedoes that struck it. But internal explosions eventually brought it down, and the men were forced to abandon ship.

The death of the *Lexington* was a terrible blow for the U.S. Navy. But the Battle of the Coral Sea was widely seen as a success because it prevented the Japanese from landing at Port Moresby. The Japanese called off the invasion, retreated, and said they would return later. Actually, no other attempt was ever made to take the city. Port Moresby became a major base for General MacArthur when, later in 1942, he began the long campaign that took him back to the Philippines.

■ ■ ■

The air attack at New Guinea, the Doolittle raid, and the Battle of the Coral Sea were all minor victories that lifted the spirits of the American people. But soon there was to be a major U.S. victory far to the north in the Pacific.

FIVE: THE BATTLE OF MIDWAY

The commander of the Japanese Navy, Admiral Isoroko Yamamoto, had planned and led the attack on Pearl Harbor. In May 1942, he began planning a new operation. It was to take place some 1,300 miles north of Hawaii and called for a vast fleet to attack and capture the small island of Midway.

Yamamoto intended to do much more than take the American-owned island, which his forces had bypassed in the Pearl Harbor attack. What he really had in mind was the destruction of the remaining ships in the U.S. Pacific Fleet. He was certain they would race to Midway from their headquarters at Hawaii. His giant armada would then sink them.

Yamamoto had never wanted to go to war with the United States. He had struck Pearl Harbor on orders from his superiors in Tokyo and had worried that his country was making a terrible mistake.

He was also worried about the possible results of the Pearl Harbor assault. Although it had destroyed many U.S. ships, it had left many more in fighting condition. These ships would soon be joined by others now being built in U.S. shipyards. Together, he knew, they could take control of the Pacific. The enemy's back must be broken immediately if Japan hoped to retain its hold on the Pacific.

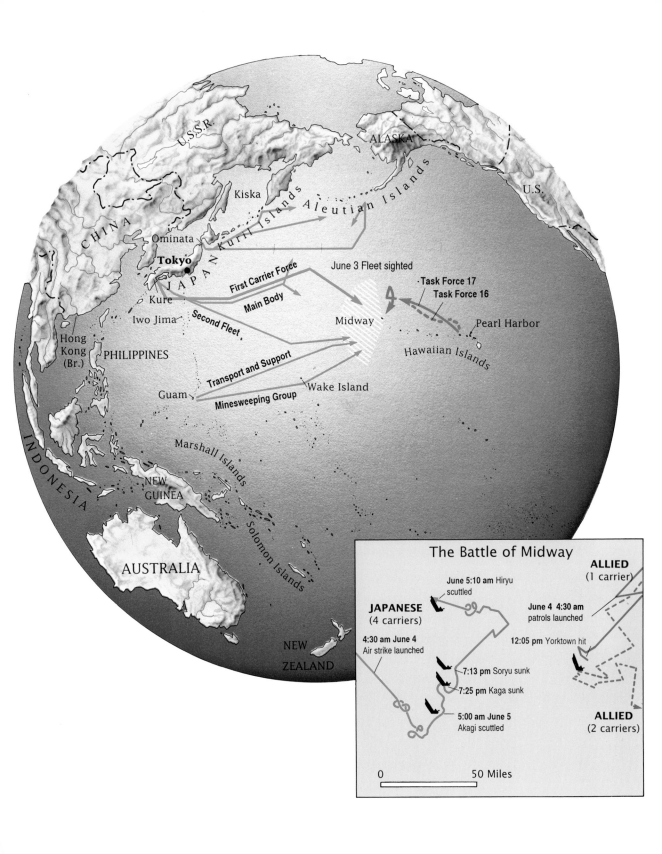

CHINA

U.S.S.R.

ALASKA

U.S.

Kiska

Kurill Islands

Aleutian Islands

Ominata

Tokyo

JAPAN

June 3 Fleet sighted

Task Force 17

Task Force 16

First Carrier Force

Kure

Main Body

Midway

Pearl Harbor

Iwo Jima

Second Fleet

Hawaiian Islands

Hong Kong (Br.)

PHILIPPINES

Transport and Support

Guam

Minesweeping Group

Wake Island

Marshall Islands

NEW GUINEA

INDONESIA

AUSTRALIA

Solomon Islands

NEW ZEALAND

The Battle of Midway

June 5:10 am Hiryu scuttled

JAPANESE
(4 carriers)

ALLIED
(1 carrier)

June 4 4:30 am patrols launched

4:30 am June 4
Air strike launched

12:05 pm Yorktown hit

7:13 pm Soryu sunk

7:25 pm Kaga sunk

5:00 am June 5
Akagi scuttled

ALLIED
(2 carriers)

0   50 Miles

Yamamoto assembled a fleet of more than two hundred warships and put them to sea in late May. Some were to sail to the Aleutian Islands off the coast of Alaska and stage an invasion there. According to his plan, the Americans would hurry to Alaska and be of no bother when he struck Midway.

Once he had taken Midway, his armada would lie in wait for the American ships that would now come rushing from Alaska to the real danger spot. Yamamoto had no doubt he would destroy them all. Most of the ships in the Japanese Navy would be with him. Among these were 60 destroyers, 20 cruisers, 11 battleships, and 8 carriers with more than 650 planes aboard.

ADMIRAL NIMITZ TAKES ACTION ▪ Yamamoto would not have been so sure of success had he known one fact. American cryptographers, you'll recall, had broken the code used in the Japanese war messages. Admiral Nimitz at Pearl Harbor knew all about the planned invasion of Midway.

He gathered a fleet in late May and sent a few of its ships to Alaska, with the rest heading for Midway. Bound for the island were forty-eight vessels, chief among them the carriers *Hornet, Yorktown,* and *Enterprise.* Nimitz knew his forces would be vastly outnumbered, but he had a major advantage. Yamamoto had no idea that they were out looking for him.

It seemed a miracle that the *Yorktown* was steaming to Midway. Like the *Lexington,* it had been badly damaged in the Battle of the Coral Sea. It had limped off to Hawaii and been swiftly repaired for its new assignment.

Undetected by the Japanese, the fleet sailed to a point some 250 miles northeast of Midway. There, under the command of Rear Admiral Raymond A. Spruance, it waited for Yamamoto to approach the island.

THE DAY OF FIRE AND DEATH ▪ Early on June 4, four of Yamamoto's carriers came to within two hundred miles of Midway. There were the *Akagi, Soryu, Kaga,* and *Hiryu.* The four were commanded by Admiral Chuichi Nagumo. Just before dawn, Nagumo sent out 108 planes against Midway. Their job was to bomb the island's defense installations prior to the invasion.

Although they succeeded in damaging a fuel dump and other facilities, the flight leader felt he could do more harm. He radioed Nagumo aboard the *Akagi* that another bombing attack was needed. Then he and his fellow pilots started back to their carriers.

With his bombers returning from Midway, Nagumo had only torpedo planes on his flight decks. Their missiles were suited for low-level attacks but not for bombings. He ordered his crews to replace the torpedoes with bombs for the second run over the island. The changeover would take about an hour to complete.

Astonishing news reached the admiral in the middle of the operation. One of his scout planes had sighted a large American fleet moving toward Midway. It was the first word Nagumo received of Spruance's presence in the area. Spruance had earlier learned of the bombing run on Midway and of Nagumo's location. He had immediately set his ships in motion. As soon as he came to within flying range of Nagumo's carriers, he planned to send his planes out to attack.

At a few minutes past 7 o'clock in the morning, 119 torpedo planes, dive-bombers, and fighters swept up from the *Hornet* and the *Enterprise.* They were soon followed by 35 from the *Yorktown.* They all headed straight for Nagumo's carriers—and tragedy. A protective screen of Zero fighters tore them to pieces. Most of the American planes were sent plummeting into the sea.

Nagumo was jubilant. His ships had suffered little or no damage in the attack. But then the admiral made two decisions that were to turn the tide of battle in the Americans' favor. First, he reversed the order to arm his torpedo planes with bombs and called for them to be fitted again with torpedoes. Next, instead of immediately hitting Spruance with the torpedo planes that still carried their regular missiles, he held them back while he allowed the bombers returning from Midway to land.

These actions gave the American admiral time to get fifty more dive-bombers into the air. Out of their hiding place in the clouds, they suddenly swooped down on Nagumo's carriers. His mouth gaped as they came screaming through a screen of Zeroes and headed for his *Akagi* and the nearby *Kaga* and *Soryu*. Seconds later, a bomb tore a huge hole in the *Akagi*'s flight deck. Bombs stored there began to explode, and fire swept through the entire ship.

REAR ADM. RAYMOND A. SPRUANCE

Spruance commanded the American fleet in the Battle of Midway. The fleet, which would have been led by Admiral William Halsey, went to Spruance when Halsey was hospitalized in Hawaii to recuperate from a skin infection.

Facing page: U. S. Navy dive bombers attack the Japanese fleet off Midway in June 1942. Far left: Japanese Navy admiral Isoroko Yamamoto, planner of the Pearl Harbor attack, died in April 1943, when his aircraft was attacked and shot down while en route to the Solomon Islands. Left: Japanese Admiral Chuichi Nagumo.

A Japanese cruiser takes a hit during the Battle of Midway.

The *Kaga* and *Soryu* each suffered the same fate. Bomb hits started a fire that burned into the *Kaga*'s ammunition magazine and set off a series of explosions that destroyed the ship. Likewise the *Soryu* was turned into a blazing, useless torch.

Nagumo had lost three of his finest carriers. His fourth, the *Hiryu,* escaped harm because it was located some miles away. The ship immediately launched a squadron of planes against Spruance. They found the *Yorktown* and sent three bombs slamming into it. One hurtled down its smokestack, knocked out five boilers, and left the ship lying dead in the water. Then more enemy planes arrived. Two torpedoes blasted open the ship's sides. Water gushed through the openings. The *Yorktown* began to list, but somehow the crew kept it afloat.

Pilots from the *Enterprise* soon avenged the wounded ship. They sighted the *Hiryu.* Moments later, it was on its way to the bottom. All of Nagumo's carriers were now lost.

Late in the day, on a ship far to the west, Admiral Yamamoto received word of the Nagumo disaster. He ordered his battleships to speed toward Midway for an attack on Spruance that night. Under the cover of darkness, their long-distance shells would rip the Americans to pieces. But Spruance, sensing what was coming, refused to endanger his ships in a fight with the gigantic battlewagons. He ordered his fleet to escape eastward.

The next morning, Yamamoto realized that he would never catch the retreating Spruance. He ordered a return to Japan. Midway remained out of Japanese hands for the remainder of the war. As for the Aleutians, a small Japanese force landed on two of the islands—Attu and Kiska. The presence of the

The *USS Yorktown* is bombed during the Battle of Midway.

enemy off the mainland of Alaska triggered fears that the Japanese might try to invade the United States itself. These fears came to nothing. Attu and Kiska remained as useless enemy outposts until they were retaken in 1943.

The Battle of Midway was a big defeat for Yamamoto. It cost him four carriers, a cruiser, more than 322 aircraft, and the lives of over 3,000 men. In comparison, the Americans lost the *Yorktown,* the destroyer *Hammann,* 147 planes, and 307 men.

The *Yorktown* had been taken in tow by the *Hammann* at the end of the battle and was being brought back to Hawaii for repairs when an enemy submarine sighted it. A series of torpedoes destroyed the two ships.

The Battle of Midway was more than a defeat for Yamamoto. It left the Japanese Navy crippled and was to go down in history as a turning point in the war. From that point on, the Americans would be on the offensive, driving the Japanese out of their Pacific bases and pushing them back toward their homeland.

SIX:
THE WAR IN EUROPE

What was happening in the war with Germany and Italy during the battle for the Philippines and the first American successes against the Japanese?

There was intense fighting in both Russia and North Africa. The fighting in Russia had begun in 1941, when Hitler sent a massive force thundering across its borders. By early 1942, the Germans were thrusting deep into the Russian interior.

The North African fighting began in 1940. It was then that Italian dictator Benito Mussolini decided to try to take possession of Egypt so that he and Germany's Hitler would have access to the rich oil deposits of the Mideast. Mussolini's army, however, was confronted by British and Australian troops and was soundly defeated. Hitler immediately sent forces to his aid. As 1942 dawned, tank battles were raging over hundreds of miles of desert land.

For most of 1942, except for air bombings on each other by Britain and Germany, there was little military action in western Europe. The British and Americans were quietly planning an invasion that would have them land on the coast of France for a push eastward into Germany. They hoped to launch the invasion in late 1942 or sometime in 1943.

All was not quiet, however, in the Atlantic Ocean. Throughout 1942, the ocean's northern area served as a nightmarish battleground. There, German submarines sank one Allied merchant ship after another.

THE WAR IN THE NORTH ATLANTIC ▪ Though remaining neutral at the outbreak of the European war in 1939, the United States gave aid to Britain by providing needed war supplies. Russia began receiving U.S. materials when the Germans crossed its borders in 1941. Shortly after Pearl Harbor plunged America into the war, the shipments to Britain and Russia were sharply increased.

American, British, and Russian merchant ships began ploughing continuously back and forth across the Atlantic. They took the shortest route possible—across the narrowest point of the North Atlantic.

This route held terrible dangers for the ships, especially those sailing from the United States. It required them to travel up the American eastern seaboard to the Canadian port of Halifax. From there, they set out for Britain and the Russian ports of Murmansk and Archangel, both of which stood on the nation's far northern shores.

As they moved along the eastern seaboard at night, the ships were silhouetted against the lights of the coastal cities. Six German submarines, called U-boats (Underwater boats), made their way to points off the American shore in the last days of 1941. There, they lurked quietly beneath the waves throughout the day. Then, at night, they took aim on the sharply outlined ships. In January, their torpedoes sank 42 freighters. By May, the U-boat commanders boasted a total of 87 victims.

Besides being highly visible targets, the freighters were in danger for another reason. They usually traveled alone, without a protective screen of warships to fight off the subs. This was because the United States as yet had too few vessels to serve as escorts. However, steps were soon taken to protect the freighters.

For example, they began to sail in groups called convoys. The ships in the center of each group became much harder to hit. Second, as America began producing an increasing number of warships, the convoys were given more and more escort vessels. When the convoys moved up the eastern seaboard to Halifax, they were now guarded by flotillas of U.S. Navy and Coast Guard ships. American, Canadian, British, and Russian warships accompanied them when they departed Halifax.

The added protection helped, but it did not end the slaughter being inflicted by the U-boats. Germany had earlier increased its production of the submarines, and they were now going to sea at the rate of twenty a month. Many of them gathered in groups—called "wolf packs"—at points in the North Atlantic, turning the waters there into a mass of flaming wreckage. In June alone, a record 144 Allied ships were destroyed. Yet many of the ships did get past the enemy subs and landed a growing number of supplies. They also landed the first U.S. troops that were to fight in Europe. Contingents of Americans soldiers began arriving in Ireland and England in late 1942.

The U-boats remained a menace throughout most of the war. In mid-1943, however, the tide of battle began to turn

against them. By then, fleets of warships were escorting the convoys. Improved methods of detecting the approach and position of the subs were in use. The escort ships were using effective tactics to counterattack; for example, several warships worked together to surround and destroy a sub with depth charges. In time, the North Atlantic, though still a danger spot, lost its reputation of being one of the war's bloodiest battlegrounds.

That reputation had been well deserved. Some 3,200 British merchant seamen lost their lives in the North Atlantic during the war. The American toll stood at about 6,000. Left lying on the bottom of the sea were 4,600 merchant ships and just over 750 U-boats.

THE FIRST TASTES OF BATTLE ▪ With most of the fighting in 1942 taking place in Russia and North Africa, there was not much for the U.S. troops to do when they began arriving in Ireland and Britain. A few, however, did get an early taste of battle.

The first fighting took place on July 4. A group of U.S. Army Air Force pilots celebrated their country's Independence Day by bombing a series of German airfields in the Netherlands. As yet, they had no planes of their own, so they borrowed six bombers from the British to do the job. The B-17 Flying Fortresses and B-24 Liberators that would later enable the Americans to join the British in bombing raids against Germany were just beginning to be produced in great numbers back home. Months would pass before they would begin arriving in Britain.

The Americans had their second taste of battle in August. Fifty U.S. Army Rangers (commando fighters) joined a force

Troop transports with escorts crossing the North Atlantic.

of 5,000 Canadians and 1,000 British in a guerrilla-type raid against the French port city of Dieppe. The city lay just sixty-five miles across the English Channel from Britain.

The raid, which bore the code name Operation Jubilee, was made as part of the planning for the anticipated invasion of France. It was meant to test the defense installations that the Germans had built all along the French coast since taking over the country in 1940. Dieppe was picked for the raid because it was seen as a possible site for the invasion.

On the night of August 19, the raiders silently landed on the coast. In the next hours, they met with both success and tragedy. On the one hand, a group that struck a nearby German airfield destroyed 58 parked planes. However, the raiders were soon overwhelmed by the large German force that guarded the seaport. Some 2,000 raiders were captured and taken prisoner, and another 1,000 were killed.

OPERATION TORCH ▪ The next taste of battle for the Americans came in November. This time, however, they received more than just a taste. Some 84,000 U.S. troops and 23,000 British took part in Operation TORCH.

Operation TORCH was a military action meant to replace the plan to strike at Germany by invading France. It took shape when the invasion planners decided that the French coast was too heavily fortified for an attack. Instead, they decided to strike North Africa.

The newly planned invasion had several goals. First, the British and Americans believed that once North Africa was under their control, they could use it as a base for a future assault on what Winston Churchill, the prime minister of

Britain, called the "soft underbelly of Europe." They could cross the Mediterranean Sea to invade Italy and then advance north to sections of France and Germany that were not as strongly defended as the French west coast. Second, by taking North Africa from the Germans and Italians, they could remove the threat of the enemy having access to the oil resources of the Mideast.

Operation TORCH was launched on November 8, 1942, under the command of the U.S. Army's General Dwight D. Eisenhower. American and British troops stormed ashore at points along a stretch of coastline that extended from the country of Morocco on the west to its neighbor, Algeria, on the east.

The battle for North Africa would rage until the Allies would finally win it in the following year. Because so much of the fighting took place in 1943, Operation TORCH will be more fully described in the next book in this series—*America in World War II: 1943.*

GEN. DWIGHT D. EISENHOWER

For a time in the 1930s, the man who was destined to become president of the United States served as a major on General MacArthur's staff in the Philippines. He was later appointed Chief of Staff of the Third Army Corps and then sent to England in 1942 with the rank of lieutenant general to plan U.S.-British military operations. He led Operation TORCH in North Africa and became the commander of the European theater of operations.

SEVEN: THE UNITED STATES IN 1942

The year 1942 was one of mixed emotions for the American people. It was a year of sad farewells and feelings of pride as 4 million men and women entered the military service, some as volunteers, others as draftees. In time, more than 16 million of the nation's citizens would be in uniform.

Adding to the sadness in the early part of the year was the news from Bataan and Corregidor. Later, word of the battles of the Coral Sea and Midway brought more mixed emotions—sadness at the loss of the *Lexington* and the *Yorktown* and so many of their crewman but also elation that the country was beginning to strike back at the Japanese.

There was one emotion, however, that did not change throughout the entire year. It was the angry determination to avenge Pearl Harbor and win the war. That determination was clearly demonstrated by America's workers and industries.

For months before the attack on Pearl Harbor, the United States had been supplying Great Britain, Russia, and China with war materials. At that time, President Roosevelt had promised that his nation would serve as the ''arsenal of democracy.''

Assembly-line workers at a Midwestern munitions plant turning out antitank shells.

The country now began to make Roosevelt's promise come true. It plunged into the work of providing itself and its fellow Allied nations with the tools of war. Everywhere, factories switched from the manufacture of peacetime goods to the production of arms.

Just how many people went to work in the war industries? The number rose steadily throughout 1942 until it stood close to the 20 million mark at year's end. Women—14 million in all—made up a major percentage of that number. They worked because they wanted to help and because they were needed to replace the men entering the armed services.

The United States was ideally suited for the massive job it took on. In peacetime years, it had developed efficient methods for the mass production of merchandise; those methods were now put to use to turn out wartime goods. Further, it had a huge labor force and was located far from the war zones.

Considering that the early months were spent gearing up for wartime work, the nation's industries did well in 1942. Along with all the rifles, tanks, trucks, jeeps, freighters, and warships that took shape, some 47,000 new warplanes rolled off the assembly lines. In all, by year's end, the United States was turning out more military goods than were Germany, Italy, and Japan put together.

The federal government supervised the production. It established a number of agencies to handle this task. One agency, the War Production Board, was created to deal with any problem that hampered the flow of goods.

Not all the production took place in industry. American scientists began to work on some new and exciting projects, among them radar, magnetic mines, rockets, guided missiles, and jet propulsion. In many of their efforts, the Americans worked closely with British researchers; Britain at the time was far ahead of the United States in the development of such tools of war as radar. Out of U.S. laboratories also came new drugs for the treatment of wounds and diseases. And, when the country ran short of rubber after one of its chief suppliers—the Malayan peninsula—fell to the Japanese, the labs devised a synthetic rubber to take its place.

In December 1942, one of the most significant scientific experiments in history realized its first success. In secret, scientists at the University of Chicago achieved an atomic chain reaction. America was on its way to building the atomic bombs that would bring the war with Japan to a sudden close in 1945 and plunge humankind into the Atomic Age.

A PEOPLE AT WAR ▪ As the year passed, Americans everywhere slowly became accustomed to the idea of being at war. They closely followed the news of the fighting overseas. They learned to live without all the gasoline they had once been able to buy for their cars. Gasoline was now being rationed so that most of it could go where it was most needed. It was also rationed to keep people from driving too much and wearing out their tires since rubber was in short supply and needed for the war effort.

People did whatever they could to assist the war effort. Many planned recreational activities for the uniformed men and women who dropped in at YMCA, YWCA, Red Cross, church, and USO (United Service Organization) facilities across the country. Others packaged food and clothing for people overseas. Americans everywhere purchased U.S. War Bonds to help finance the costs of the war.

In all, 1942 was a year that gave Americans a deep sense of pride. Only one incident triggered a feeling of shame in some that year, and in many others in later years. It concerned the 111,000 Japanese-Americans who were living in the United States. About two thirds were U.S. citizens, and most lived on the Pacific coast.

Officials in California and Washington feared that these people would turn traitor in the event of an invasion and act as spies and saboteurs for the enemy. To offset this possibility, Japanese-American men, women, and children were taken from their homes, businesses, and schools and herded together in camps located in some of the country's most remote areas. They remained there for most of the war years.

These actions were really a result of the war hysteria that so often accompanies the early days of fighting. Especially in the later years, they were seen as a violation of the civil rights of the imprisoned Japanese-Americans. People also thought it a foolish step because they felt most Japanese-Americans were loyal to the United States and because many of the imprisoned were so young or so old that they could not possibly be threats to the nation.

Later in the war, an army contingent of young Japanese-Americans served with distinction overseas. In still later years, the imprisoned Japanese-Americans were given some financial compensation for the losses they had suffered on being sent to the camps.

The year 1942 ended on a high note for Americans everywhere when, in November, they received word that U.S. forces were striking at Hitler and Mussolini by invading North Africa. Even earlier, there had been hopeful words from the

Japanese Americans were evacuated to internment camps, where most would remain for the duration of the war.

Pacific. On August 7, the press reported that General MacArthur was at last embarking on the campaign that would carry him back to the Philippines. His forces were invading the island of Guadalcanal, near the southern end of the Solomon Islands. This invasion marked the first step in the retaking of the Solomons, which the Japanese had seized in March. It seemed to the people at home that the time of defeat that had followed Pearl Harbor had come to an end. Their country was now on the march.

BIBLIOGRAPHY

Associated Press, *World War II: A 50th Anniversary History*. New York: Holt, 1989.

Bailey, Thomas A. *The American Pageant: A History of the Republic*. Boston: D. C. Heath, 1956.

Burke, Merle. *United States History: The Growth of Our Land*. Chicago: American Technical Society, 1957.

Flanagan, Lt. Gen. E. M. *Corregidor: The Rock Force Assault, 1945*. Novato, California: Presidio Press, 1988.

Gilbert, Martin. *The Second World War: A Complete History*. New York: Holt, 1989.

Hall, John Whitney, ed. *History of the World: World War I to the Present Day*. Greenwich, Connecticut: Bison Books, 1988.

Lawson, Don. *The United States in World War II*. New York: Abelard-Schuman, 1963.

Macdonald, John. *Great Battles of World War II*. New York: Macmillan, 1986.

Morison, Samuel Eliot, and Henry Steele Commager. *The Growth of the American Republic, 1865–1950*. New York: Oxford University Press, 1950.

Steinberg, Rafael, and the editors of Time-Life Books. *Return to the Philippines*. Alexandria, Virginia: Time-Life Books, 1979.

Sulzberger, C. L. *The American Heritage Picture History of World War II*. New York: American Heritage Publishing, 1966.

Toland, John. *But Not in Shame: The Six Months After Pearl Harbor*. New York: Random House, 1976.

_____. *The Rising Sun: The Decline and Fall of the Japanese Empire, 1936–1945*. New York: Random House, 1970.

Zich, Arthur, and the editors of Time-Life Books. *The Rising Sun*. Alexandria, Virginia: Time-Life Books, 1979.

INDEX